Jazz PLAY ALONG

Book and CD for B♭, E♭ and C Instruments

volume 35

Bluesy Jazz

T0058942

BOOK

10 Jazz Favorites

CD

ISBN 978-0-634-07990-0

HAL•LEONARD® CORPORATION

7777 W. BLUEMOUND RD. P.O. BOX 13819 MILWAUKEE, WI 53213

Visit Hal Leonard Online at
www.halleonard.com

Bluesy Jazz

Volume 35

Arranged and Produced by
Mark Taylor

Featured Players:

Graham Breedlove-Trumpet
John Desalme-Tenor Sax
Tony Nalker-Piano
Jim Roberts-Bass
Steve Fidyk-Drums

HOW TO USE THE CD:

Each song has <u>two</u> tracks:

1) Split Track/Melody

Woodwind, Brass, Keyboard, and Mallet Players can use this track as a learning tool for melody style and inflection.

Bass Players can learn and perform with this track – remove the recorded bass track by turning down the volume on the LEFT channel.

Keyboard and **Guitar Players** can learn and perform with this track – remove the recorded piano part by turning down the volume on the RIGHT channel.

2) Full Stereo Track

Soloists or **Groups** can learn and perform with this accompaniment track with the RHYTHM SECTION only.

ANGEL EYES

CD
❶ : SPLIT TRACK/MELODY
❷ : FULL STEREO TRACK

C VERSION

WORDS BY EARL BRENT
MUSIC BY MATT DENNIS

BAGS' GROOVE

C VERSION

BY MILT JACKSON

BESSIE'S BLUES

BY JOHN COLTRANE

CD
◆ 5 : SPLIT TRACK/MELODY
◆ 6 : FULL STEREO TRACK

C VERSION

CHITLINS CON CARNE

GOOD MORNING HEARTACHE

WORDS AND MUSIC BY DAN FISHER,
IRENE HIGGINBOTHAM AND ERVIN DRAKE

C VERSION

HIGH FLY

C VERSION

BY RANDY WESTON

MERCY, MERCY, MERCY

CD
13 : SPLIT TRACK/MELODY
14 : FULL STEREO TRACK

COMPOSED BY JOSEF ZAWINUL

C VERSION

Night Train

SUGAR

BY STANLEY TURRENTINE

C VERSION

SWEET GEORGIA BRIGHT

CD
19 : SPLIT TRACK/MELODY
20 : FULL STEREO TRACK

C VERSION

BY CHARLES LLOYD

ANGEL EYES

WORDS BY EARL BRENT
MUSIC BY MATT DENNIS

17

CD
◆ 3 : SPLIT TRACK/MELODY
◆ 4 : FULL STEREO TRACK

BAGS' GROOVE

Bb VERSION

BY MILT JACKSON

MEDIUM SWING

BESSIE'S BLUES

BY JOHN COLTRANE

CHITLINS CON CARNE

BY KENNY BURRELL

GOOD MORNING HEARTACHE

WORDS AND MUSIC BY DAN FISHER,
IRENE HIGGINBOTHAM AND ERVIN DRAKE

HIGH FLY

BY RANDY WESTON

MERCY, MERCY, MERCY

Bb VERSION

COMPOSED BY JOSEF ZAWINUL

SLOW FUNKY ROCK

Night Train

CD
- ◆15: SPLIT TRACK/MELODY
- ◆16: FULL STEREO TRACK

WORDS BY OSCAR WASHINGTON
& LEWIS C. SIMPKINS
MUSIC BY JIMMY FORREST

SUGAR

Bb VERSION

BY STANLEY TURRENTINE

Sweet Georgia Bright

Bb VERSION

BY CHARLES LLOYD

ANGEL EYES

WORDS BY EARL BRENT
MUSIC BY MATT DENNIS

CD
1: SPLIT TRACK/MELODY
2: FULL STEREO TRACK

Eb VERSION   SLOW

CD
❸ : SPLIT TRACK/MELODY
❹ : FULL STEREO TRACK

BAGS' GROOVE

BY MILT JACKSON

BESSIE'S BLUES

BY JOHN COLTRANE

GOOD MORNING HEARTACHE

WORDS AND MUSIC BY DAN FISHER,
IRENE HIGGINBOTHAM AND ERVIN DRAKE

HIGH FLY

MERCY, MERCY, MERCY

COMPOSED BY JOSEF ZAWINUL

Eb VERSION

Night Train

WORDS BY OSCAR WASHINGTON
& LEWIS C. SIMPKINS
MUSIC BY JIMMY FORREST

CD
15 : SPLIT TRACK/MELODY
16 : FULL STEREO TRACK

Eb VERSION

SUGAR

CD

17 : SPLIT TRACK/MELODY
18 : FULL STEREO TRACK

Eb VERSION

BY STANLEY TURRENTINE

SWEET GEORGIA BRIGHT

CD
19 : SPLIT TRACK/MELODY
20 : FULL STEREO TRACK

Eb VERSION

BY CHARLES LLOYD

ANGEL EYES

WORDS BY EARL BRENT
MUSIC BY MATT DENNIS

BAGS' GROOVE

BY MILT JACKSON

9: C VERSION

BESSIE'S BLUES

BY JOHN COLTRANE

℃: C VERSION

CHITLINS CON CARNE

GOOD MORNING HEARTACHE

WORDS AND MUSIC BY DAN FISHER,
IRENE HIGGINBOTHAM AND ERVIN DRAKE

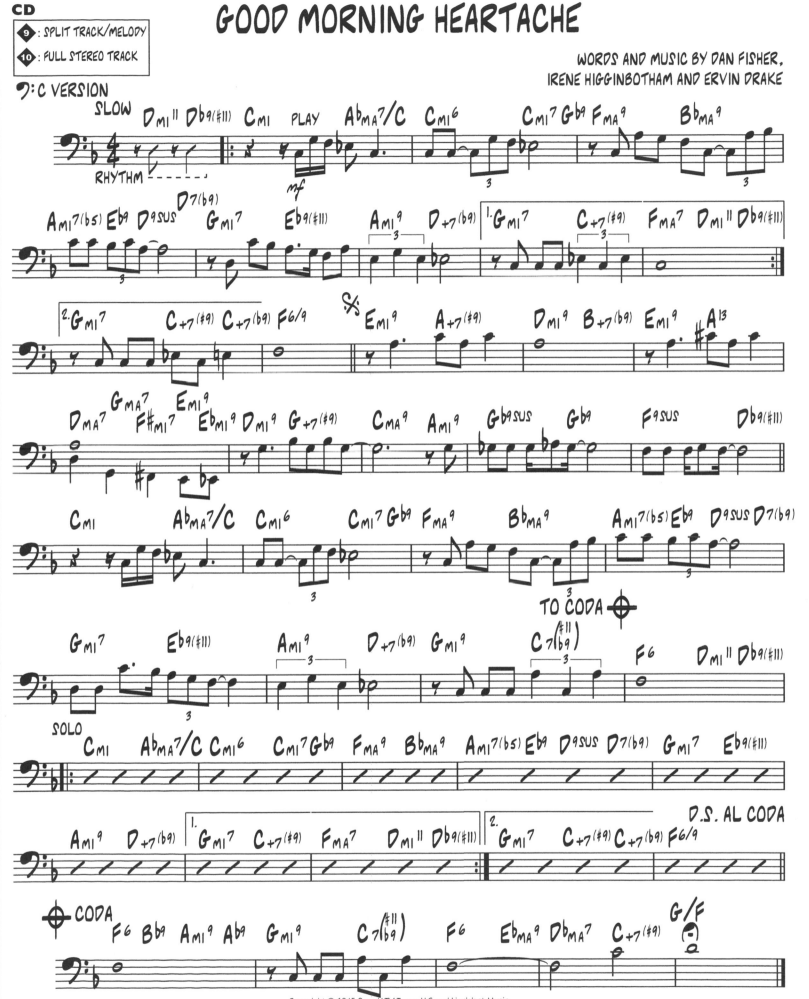

HIGH FLY

CD
11 : SPLIT TRACK/MELODY
12 : FULL STEREO TRACK

𝄢: C VERSION

BY RANDY WESTON

MERCY, MERCY, MERCY

COMPOSED BY JOSEF ZAWINUL

Night Train

WORDS BY OSCAR WASHINGTON
& LEWIS C. SIMPKINS
MUSIC BY JIMMY FORREST

SUGAR

SWEET GEORGIA BRIGHT

BY CHARLES LLOYD